Key Stage 2 LEARN Spelling

Contents

AUTHOR: Camilla de la Bédoyère
EDITORIAL: Catherine de la Bédoyère, Quentin de la Bédoyère, John Bolt, Vicky Garrard, Kate Lawson, Sally MacGill, Julia Rolf, Lyndall Willis
DESIGN: Jen Bishop, Dave Jones, Colin Rudderham
ILLUSTRATORS: David Benham, Sarah Wimperis
PRODUCTION: Chris Herbert, Claire Walker
Thanks also to Robert Walster

COMMISSIONING EDITOR: Polly Willis
PUBLISHER AND CREATIVE DIRECTOR: Nick Wells

3 Book Pack ISBN 1-84451-052-2   Book ISBN 1-84451-033-6
6 Book Pack ISBN 1-84451-066-2   Book ISBN 1-84451-080-8
First published in 2003

A copy of the CIP data for this book is available from the British Library upon request.

Created and produced by
FLAME TREE PUBLISHING
Crabtree Hall,
Crabtree Lane,
Fulham, London SW6 6TY
United Kingdom
www.flametreepublishing.com

Flame Tree Publishing is part of The Foundry Creative Media Co. Ltd.

© The Foundry Creative Media Co. Ltd, 2003

Printed in Croatia

Foreword

Sometimes when I am crossing the playground on my way to visit a primary school I pass young children playing at schools. There is always a stern authoritarian little teacher at the front laying down the law to the unruly group of children in the pretend class. This puzzles me a little because the school I am visiting is very far from being like the children's play. Where do they get this Victorian view of what school is like? Perhaps it's handed down from generation to generation through the genes. Certainly they don't get it from their primary school. Teachers today are more often found alongside their pupils, who are learning by actually doing things for themselves, rather than merely listening and obeying instructions.

Busy children, interested and involved in their classroom reflect what we know about how they learn. Of course they learn from teachers but most of all they learn from their experience of life and their life is spent both in and out of school. Indeed, if we compare the impact upon children of even the finest schools and teachers, we find that three or four times as great an impact is made by the reality of children's lives outside the school. That reality has the parent at the all important centre. No adult can have so much impact, for good or ill, as the young child's mother or father.

This book, and others in the series, are founded on the sure belief that the great majority of parents want to help their children grow and learn and that teachers are keen to support them. The days when parents were kept at arm's length from schools are long gone and over the years we have moved well beyond the white line painted on the playground across which no parent must pass without an appointment. Now parents move freely in and out of schools and very often are found in the classrooms backing up the teachers. Both sides of the partnership know how important it is that children should be challenged and stimulated both in and out of school.

Perhaps the most vital part of this book is where parents and children are encouraged to develop activities beyond those offered on the page. The more the children explore and use the ideas and techniques we want them to learn, the more they will make new knowledge of their very own. It's not just getting the right answer, it's growing as a person through gaining skill in action and not only in books. The best way to learn is to live.

I remember reading a story to a group of nine year old boys. The story was about soldiers and of course the boys, bloodthirsty as ever, were hanging on my every word. I came to the word khaki and I asked the group "What colour is khaki?" One boy was quick to answer. "Silver" he said, "It's silver." "Silver? I queried. "Yes," he said with absolute confidence, "silver, my Dad's car key is silver." Now I reckon I'm a pretty good teller of stories to children but when it came down to it, all my dramatic reading of a gripping story gave way immediately to the power of the boy's experience of life. That meant so much more to him, as it does to all children.

JOHN COE
General Secretary
National Association for Primary Education (NAPE).

NAPE was founded 23 years ago with the aim of improving the quality of teaching and learning in primary schools. The association brings together parents and teachers in partnership.

NAPE, Moulton College, Moulton, Northampton, NN3 7RR, Telephone: 01604 647 646 Web: www. nape.org.uk

Spelling is one of six books in the **Learn** series, which has been devised to help you support your child through Key Stage Two.

The National Literacy Strategy Framework recognises that teachers have often been over-cautious about the teaching of phonics (sounds) and spelling. Yet research shows that children do not learn to identify the sounds of words simply by reading; they need to be taught to do this. The Framework states that it is essential that children are taught basic decoding and spelling skills and **Spelling** aims to help you achieve this. This book contains spelling rules that your child will be expected to know by the end of Year Four.

Daily reading, of both fiction and non-fiction, will further develop a sound understanding of texts and will contribute to the organisation and accuracy of your child's work.

Each page contains exercises for your child to complete, an activity they can complete away from book and **Parents Start Here** boxes to give you extra information and guidance. At the end of the book you will find a checklist of topics – you can use this to mark off each topic as it is mastered.

This book has been designed so your child can work through most sections alone, however there are dictation exercises (with full instructions) that you need to read to your child and mark. It is recommended that you read the book first to acquaint yourself with the material it contains. Try to be at hand when your child is working with the book; your input is valuable.

Encourage good study habits in your child:

- Try to set aside a short time every day for studying. 10 to 20 minutes a day is plenty.

- Establish a quiet and comfortable environment for your child to work and suitable tools e.g. sharp pencils and good handwriting pens. Your child will need a dictionary to complete some sections of this book.

- Give your child access to drinking water whenever they work; research suggests this helps them perform better.

- Reward your child; plenty of praise for good work motivates children to succeed.

- Ensure your child eats a healthy diet, gets plenty of rest and lots of opportunity to play.

This book is intended to support your child in their school work. Some children find spelling particularly difficult; you should discuss this with their teacher who may suggest seeking specialist help.

Your child will need a dictionary and a good handwriting pen or pencil.

Top Tip! Don't worry if your child does not understand straightaway – children learn at different speeds.

Parents Start Here...

Find out if your child has access to drinking water throughout the day at school. If not, find out why. There is plenty of evidence that children who drink water whenever they are thirsty perform better at school.

How To Spell

Some people find spelling really easy, some people find spelling really tough. Most people find spelling quite tricky sometimes.

One of the big problems with spelling is that while some words are dead easy to read and spell (such as cat, dog and hop) some words just don't look like they sound e.g. pneumatic, knowledge and pseudonym.

The bad news is that you just have to get on and learn how to spell and that means a lot of work.

The good news is that there are lots of spelling rules that can help make sense of some of the weirder words. There are also clever tricks that you can use to get the hang of the worst ones.

Here are some **Top Spelling Tips:**

- Learn the Spelling Rules and learn the exceptions to the rules.

   (We'll go through lots of rules in this book.)

- Divide the words into chunks (syllables) and say them out loud.

   e.g. introspection ➡ in/tro/spec/tion

- There are some words you just have to learn off by heart, by spelling them out, one letter at a time:

   e.g. thorough ➡ t-h-o-r-o-u-g-h

- Use your body to help you spell:

  - Use your eyes to look at the word. Look for double letters, special endings or anything unusual.

  - Use your tongue to say the word in syllables.

  - Use your ears to listen to the sounds of the syllables and letters.

  - Use your brain to remember the spelling rules and think about the word's meaning.

  - Use your hands. Write words in the air, using your fingers. Keep your movements large, fluid and write in joined-up writing.

  - Use your legs to march while you learn your spellings. Every time you say a letter you can try marching on the spot, or tapping your head – whatever works for you.

- Use the Look, Say, Cover, Write and Check method of learning your spellings. We'll go through this later on.

And finally,

Look after your **brain**:

1. Drink a glass of water when you get up in the morning. Drink plenty of water throughout the day, not just with meals.

2. Eat a healthy diet that is balanced and has plenty of proteins, carbohydrates and fats.

3. Exercise every day and get enough sleep.

Activity

Practise your joined-up writing by seeing if you can write from a to z without taking your pen off the page. You can cross your t and dot your i and j when you have finished.

Check Your Progress!

How To Spell

Turn to page 48 and put a tick next to what you have just learned.

Parents Start Here...

Research suggests that joining up all the letters in a word helps children learn to spell. Encourage continuous, flowing handwriting.

Spelling With –ing And –le

Verbs can be changed by adding –ing to them:

I run to school. ➡ I was running to school.

The Rule: When the verb ends in a vowel – consonant we need to double the consonant:

hop ➡ hopping

skip ➡ _____

shop ➡ _____

The alphabet contains 26 letters; a e i o u are vowels and all the rest are consonants, except for y, which sometimes behaves like a vowel and sometimes behaves like a consonant.

The Rule: When the verb ends in an –e we take off the –e then add –ing:

like ➡ liking

make ➡ _____

pile ➡ _____

The Rule: When the verb ends in two consonants you can just add the –ing:

tick ➡ ticking

mark ➡ _____

rest ➡ _____

The Rule: Words that end in –le sometimes have double consonants before the –le:

For example: battle   puzzle   bottle

Write the name: _____

Write the name: _____

Write the name _____

The letter pattern in these words makes the vowel sound short. This means that the a in battle says its sound, not its name. Say the vowel sounds for the u in puzzle and o in bottle.

Exceptions: Words that end in –ble e.g. crumble, humble, scramble, able, table.

There are other exceptions too e.g. needle, chuckle, bundle and example.

Home Learn

Write the following words out in joined up handwriting. Try not to lift the pen or pencil from the beginning to the end of each word:

muddle _____   bottle _____

kettle _____   apple _____

ripple _____

Activity

TRY THIS

Think of three nouns that end in –ing. (A noun is a place, name or thing.)

Check Your Progress!
Spelling With –ing And –le
Turn to page 48 and put a tick next to what you have just learned.

7

Top Tip! Go through this page as often as you like until your child understands it fully.

Parents Start Here...

Children are expected to use their knowledge of prefixes to generate new words from root words, especially antonyms (opposites).

Common Prefixes

A prefix is a group of letters that can go at the front of a word. A prefix changes the meaning of the word:

comfortable	➡	uncomfortable	the prefix is un
like	➡	dislike	the prefix is dis
cycle	➡	_____	the prefix is re
code	➡	decode	the prefix is _____

Here is a Look, Say, Cover, Write and Check Chart for you to fill in.

Step One Look at the word, say the word.	Step Two Cover the word, write it then check it.	Step Three Cover the word, write it then check it.
usual		
unusual		
appear		
disappear		
play		
replay		
like		
dislike		
wind		
rewind		

You can use prefixes to make your own words.

Add prefixes:

happy ➡ opposite of happy ➡ _____

tidy ➡ opposite of tidy ➡ _____

lucky ➡ opposite of lucky ➡ _____

Happy, tidy and lucky are all root words.

Home Learn

Here are some other common prefixes. Think of a root word for each and write it down, using joined-up handwriting.

For example:

dis + qualify	➡	disqualify
anti + _____	➡	_____
non + _____	➡	_____
im + _____	➡	_____
in + _____	➡	_____

Activity

Check your pencil grip. If you are holding your pencil too tight it will be difficult to pull it out of your grasp with your other hand.

Check Your Progress!
Common Prefixes

Turn to page 48 and put a tick next to what you have just learned.

Parents Start Here...

Encourage your child to think of other examples that obey these spelling rules.

Changing Words

A suffix is a group of letters that is added to the end of words. A suffix changes the meaning of a word:

Adding –er and –est

We can use the suffix –er to mean 'more' of something:

tall   ➡   taller

bright   ➡   _____

We can use the suffix –est to mean 'most' of something:

tall   ➡   tallest

bright   ➡   _____

Some words have to change before these suffixes can be added:

The Rule: If a word ends in –e, remove the –e, before–er or –est:

nice   ➡   nicer   ➡   nicest

close   ➡   closer   ➡   _____

The Rule: If a word ends in –y, replace the –y with -i, before –er or –est:

lucky   ➡   luckier   ➡   luckiest

pretty   ➡   prettier   ➡   _____

Adding –y

We can add –y to some nouns to turn them into adjectives:

The chocolate bar has milk in it.

The chocolate bar is milky.

> Remember: a noun names a place, person or thing. An adjective describes a noun.

It is not so simple with all nouns:

> **The Rule:** If the vowel before the last consonant says its sound rather than its name, you need to double the consonant before you add the –y.

the u says its sound

run ➡ double the consonant ➡ runn ➡ add the y ➡ runny

sun ➡ double the consonant ➡ ____ ➡ add the y ➡ _____

> **The Rule:** If the word ends in –e, take the –e off before adding the –y

stone ➡ stony   shine ➡ shiny

Home Learn

Add –y to the ends of these words, following the rules:

milk ➡ _____

star ➡ _____

skin ➡ _____

fur ➡ _____

grease ➡ _____

Activity

Every time you write, check your feet are flat on the ground and your bottom is near the back of your chair.

> ### Check Your Progress!
> ### Changing Words ☐
> Turn to page 48 and put a tick next to what you have just learned.

Parents Start Here...

The National Literacy Strategy sets outs the need for children to understand the sound and spelling system, and use this to read and spell accurately.

Writing Plurals

I have one friend. ——— there is only one friend: this word is singular

I have lots of friends. ——— there is more than one friend; this word is plural

When we make a word into a plural we usually just add −s.

train ➡ trains

car ➡ cars

mate ➡ _____

Some words need to have the suffix −es added to make them plural.

The Rule: nouns that end in −ch, -sh, -o-, -s, -x and −z need to have −es added to make the plural.

class ➡ classes

fox ➡ _____

buzz ➡ _____

wish ➡ _____

Exceptions. Just add −s:

bamboo ➡ bamboos   cockatoo ➡ cockatoos

banjo ➡ _____   piano ➡ _____

monarch ➡ _____   shampoo ➡ _____

ratio ➡ _____   radio ➡ _____

Nouns that End in –y

The Rule: if there is a vowel before the –y you can just add the –s.

birthday ➡ birthdays

Monday ➡ _____

The Rule: if there is a consonant before the –y change the –y to –i before adding –es.

nappy ➡ nappies

baby ➡ babies

butty ➡ _____

lorry ➡ _____

Home Learn

Change these nouns into plurals. Remember to use joined-up writing.

plane ➡ _____   shoe ➡ _____

ostrich ➡ _____   emu ➡ _____

church ➡ _____   key ➡ _____

lolly ➡ _____   berry ➡ _____

Activity

Look back at your joined-up writing on this page. Draw rings around the words you have written most neatly.

Check Your Progress!
Writing Plurals

Turn to page 48 and put a tick next to what you have just learned.

13

Top Tip! Bring what your child learns into everyday life – they'll remember it even better.

Parents Start Here...

Make sure your child has ready access to a dictionary and understands how to use it. We will be looking at dictionaries in more detail later. Children's dictionaries are not sufficient for this age group.

Silent Letters

The Silent K

The Rule: When you see a word beginning with kn you know that you don't say the k.

Learn these kn- words.

Look carefully at the words. Can you see any letter patterns, like 'igh', that you need to remember?

Step One Look Say	Step Two Cover Write Check	Step Three Cover Write Check
knee		
knife		
knew		
knuckle		
knead		
kneel		
knickers		
knight		

The Silent B

The Rule: When a word has –mb the b is silent.

Plumb is not the same as plum (a fruit). A plumb line is used in decorating to help you hang wallpaper.

| thumb | comb | plumb |
| plumber | lamb | climb |

The Silent G

The Rule: When you see gn– at the beginning of a word the g is silent.

Copy these words with joined-up writing:

gnome .... gnaw..............................

gnu.............................. gnash..............................

The Silent W

The Rule: When you see wr– at the beginning of a word the w is silent.

wrong   wrist   wrap   wrath   wren   wrestle

There are some other words that have a silent w:

answer   sword   whole   awkward   who

Home Learn

These words have a silent h. Write a sentence using each one of them:

why   where   when

1. _____

2. _____

3. _____

Activity

If you are not sure about the meanings of any of the words on these pages, look them up in a dictionary.

TRY THIS

Check Your Progress!

Silent Letters ☐

Turn to page 48 and put a tick next to what you have just learned.

Top Tip!
Don't worry if your child does not understand straightaway – children learn at different speeds.

Parents Start Here...

Your child will be given regular dictation sessions at school. These provide teachers with a good opportunity to test children's spellings and punctuation.

Write It Out!

1. Settle your child down comfortably. Check their writing posture is good (bottom to the back of the chair and feet on the ground).

2. Provide your child with lined writing paper and a pencil or handwriting pen, whichever your child uses at school.

3. Check your child's pencil/pen grip is correct. The pencil/pen should be held so that the child can clearly see the tip. The paper should be at a slight angle.

4. Look at the passage on the next page and ask your child to listen carefully while you read it out in a normal voice and at a normal speed.

5. Read the passage again, while your child writes it down. Read at a regular but slow pace.

6. Read the passage for a final time so you child can look at what they have written and check for mistakes.

7. When you look at your child's work you will be able to see any spellings they need to revise. Areas of weakness in punctuation will become obvious. Was your child able to write in continuous joined-up handwriting?

8. Reward your child for their efforts; plenty of praise will encourage your child to do even better next time.

9. You will find some more dictation exercises on pages 26 and 27.

The three children sat huddled around the rat. They did not know what to do with it. It looked dead, but it was hard to tell. Its little legs were sticking up in the air and its eyes were open. The cat, Tabby, was walking away looking very cross. She had been hoping to play with the rat a bit longer, but now those kids had spoiled her fun.

Practise

Write down some of the words your child had trouble spelling and ask them to practise them:

Step One Look Say	Step Two Cover Write Check	Step Three Cover Write Check

Top Tip! If your child loses concentration here, let them take a break.

Parents Start Here...

The Cross March as described in the Activity on the next page increases information flow between the left and right sides of the brain — essential for spelling, writing, listening and comprehension.

Changing The Meaning Of Words

Adding –ly

We can turn some adjectives into adverbs by simply adding –ly.

> An adjective is a word that describes a noun, an adverb is a word that describes a verb.

The cat's meow was loud.

loud describes the cat's meow

noun

The cat meowed loudly.

loudly describes the meowing

verb

Change the adjectives to adverbs:

kind ➡ _____

nice ➡ _____

quick ➡ _____

> **The Rule**: if the word ends in –y, replace the –y with –i, before adding the –ly.

happy ➡ happily

clumsy ➡ _____

nasty ➡ _____

18

Adding –less

We can change the meaning of a word by adding the suffix –less.

care ➡ careless

this means 'without care'

Change these words by adding –less and write out the new meaning. Remember to join all of the letters in each word.

thought ➡ _____

hope ➡ _____

luck ➡ _____

home ➡ _____

thank ➡ _____

Adding –ful

We can change the meaning of a word by adding the suffix –ful.

grace ➡ graceful

this means 'full of grace'

hope ➡ hopeful

thank ➡ _____

care ➡ _____

disgrace ➡ _____

Exception:

beauty ➡ beautiful

Home Learn

Write sentences using the following words:

1. (disgraceful) _____

2. (careless) _____

3. (quickly) _____

Activity

Stand up and do Cross March brain exercise. Raise your right knee and touch it with your left hand. Now raise your left knee and touch it with your right hand. Repeat 15 times.

Check Your Progress!
Changing Meanings ☐
Turn to page 48 and put a tick next to what you have just learned.

19

Top Tip!
Go through this page as often as you like until your child understands it fully.

Parents Start Here...

It is important your child understands why the English language is so complex; it is very old, but dynamic, and changes all the time.

Apostrophes

When we write some words we shorten them. We use apostrophes to show where the letters have been taken out:

we will ➡ we'll

the letters wi have been replaced with an apostrophe.

We call these shortened words contractions. It is very important that you learn how to write contractions correctly.

Here are some common contractions:

Root word	Contraction	Root word	Contraction
it is	➡ it's	I would	➡ I'd
we are	➡ we're	are not	➡ aren't
you are	➡ you're	do not	➡ don't
we will	➡ we'll	can not	➡ can't
who is	➡ who's	they are	➡ they're
you have	➡ you've	would have	➡ would've

Can you think of any more?

Exception: Here are two very odd contractions:

will not ➡ won't   shall not ➡ shan't

Top Spelling Tip

If you are not sure whether a word should have an apostrophe or not, try to turn it into the two root words. If it doesn't make sense, it isn't a contraction e.g.

ours   theirs   yours   hers   his

These words never have apostrophes.

Learn these contractions:

Step One Look Say	Step Two Cover Write Check	Step Three Cover Write Check
aren't		
weren't		
isn't		
won't		
shan't		
can't		
couldn't		
would've		
I'll		
we're		
they're		
who's		

Look carefully and decide which letters are missing in every word.

Home Learn

Write out a contraction to replace the underlined words:

a) The train would have been on time.   _____

b) I can not come to your house.   _____

c) They are not my friends any more.   _____

Activity

Contractions have come about because of the way we speak. When we talk we often join words up because they sound better, and it's quicker. Words also change from one region to another. We also get new words from other countries. Ask a grown-up to help you think of American words.

Check Your Progress!
Apostrophes ☐
Turn to page 48 and put a tick next to what you have just learned.

Parents Start Here...

Tele- is a common prefix. Help your child find other words with it, and their meanings.

Homophones

Words that sound the same, but have different spellings, are called homophones.

The Greek word homos means 'same'.

The Greek word phone means 'sound' or 'voice'.

The homophones in these sentences are circled. Write them out in the spaces below.

I went (by) bus to the shops. I waved good-(bye) to my friend then I went to (buy) some grapes.

_____

_____

_____

Here are some other homophones:

ate	➡	eight
aloud	➡	allowed
berry	➡	bury
bare	➡	bear
brake	➡	break
foul	➡	fowl
know	➡	no

Use a dictionary to find out the meanings of these homophones and then write a sentence using each of them:

a) altar
_____

alter
_____

b) dye
_____

die
_____

c) key
_____

quay
_____

d) whole
_____

hole
_____

Home Learn

Copy and complete this table by finding homophones for the words in the first columns.

	homophone			homophone
peace	_____		here	_____
plane	_____		reign	_____
bored	_____		scent	_____
sew	_____		rode	_____

Activity

Now you know how the word homophone comes from two Greek words meaning 'same sound' you may find it easier to remember. Try and find out what the 'tele' part of telephone means. Your dictionary should help.

Check Your Progress!
Homophones ☐

Turn to page 48 and put a tick next to what you have just learned.

Top Tip!
Don't worry if your child does not understand straightaway – children learn at different speeds.

Parents Start Here...

The National Literacy Strategy requires that children can identify mistakes in their own work and make the necessary corrections. Encourage your child to review their work and make improvements.

Common Letter Patterns

Vowel Sounds

The Rule: When two vowels go out walking the first one does the talking and usually says its name.

Look at these examples:

sn**ai**l	**oa**th
p**ai**l	st**oa**t
r**ai**lway	t**oa**dstool
str**ai**n	**oa**t
str**ai**ght	lifeb**oa**t
aimless	r**oa**m
cont**ai**n	

Set out words containing the sound e**a** in the same way. Here are some words to get you going:

m**ea**t _____

tr**ea**t _____

w**ea**kness _____

sp**ea**ker _____

Adding –igh

The Rule: I've got hairy toes. (-ight)

The letter pattern –igh pops up all over the place, and it often has a –t at the end. It makes the sound like the letter i when you say its name.

Learn these words:

Step One	Step Two	Step Three
Look Say	Cover Write Check	Cover Write Check
light		
bright		
sight		
sigh		
night		
knight		
right		

Have all of the words got the –ight letter pattern?

Home Learn

Copy these words using your best joined-up writing.

brightly   boastfully   faithfully

_____   _____   _____

What type of words are these?

adjectives ☐   nouns ☐   verbs ☐   adverbs ☐

TRY THIS Activity

Draw a circle around the word that you think you wrote most neatly. Ask a grown-up if they agree.

Check Your Progress! ☐
Common Letter Patterns
Turn to page 48 and put a tick next to what you have just learned.

25

Top Tip!
Learning is fun, so if your child is tired, let them come back to this when they are fresh.

Parents Start Here...

For full instructions on how to conduct the dictation exercises, refer back to pages 16 and 17.

Only do one dictation at a time.

Each dictation can be used more than once.

Correct your child's work with them; encourage them to spot their own mistakes by looking at the texts printed here.

Activities

The Magic Tree

I have a magic tree at the end of my garden. I know it's magic because the apples on it are white. There is a toadstool that grows at the foot of the tree. It's bright yellow and I think it might be magic too.

Growing Beans

Growing beans is surprisingly easy. You pop a bean in a pot of compost and water it well. Leave it in a warm, light place and add a little water every day. After only a few weeks you will see a small green shoot appear.

Crocodiles

One of the most dangerous animals in the world is the crocodile. They can eat humans but mostly they eat fish, pigs and deer. Crocodiles like to lie in the muddy waters of a river, where they wait quietly.

The Story of Jonah

In the Bible there is a story of a man, called Jonah. He got eaten by a whale. Jonah stayed alive in the whale, but after a while it spat him out. It must be strange to be inside a big animal like that.

The Pirate

Long John Silver was the pirate in the book Treasure Island. His parrot sat on his shoulder. Pirate parrots say 'pieces of eight'. Thankfully you don't come across many pirates nowadays.

My Favourite Colour

I've just had a big fight with my friend June. She says that I've always like the colour blue. I disagree with June, though. I think my favourite colour is purple, so I don't know where she got that idea from. I'll tell you one thing, my favourite person isn't June.

A Wish List

It is a good idea to write a list of all of the things you really want. It doesn't mean you're going to get them, but it's a fun thing to do. You can write down a list of things you want to do, or places you'd like to visit. Then you can try and do them all during the school holidays.

An Adventure on Spook Island

Billy, Bobby, Sally and Harry had been left on Spook Island by their wicked Uncle Timmy. The sun had nearly set and the wind blew loudly across the bay. Uncle Timmy had disappeared with the boat at 4 o'clock and night was coming fast.

Top Tip! Bring what your child learns into everyday life – they'll remember it even better.

Parents Start Here...

Whenever your child finds it hard to spell a word take them away from the book and encourage them to spell it in a different way; on a white board, in the air or even in biscuit dough.

The i Before e Rule

In most words that have the vowels i and e together, you write the i first. But when they come after c you write them the other way round. It is confusing, so there is a useful rule to help you:

The Rule: i before e, except after c, only when it rhymes with me.

These are all ie words and the ie sound rhymes with me:

> believe
> thief
> brief
> chief

Put ie into these words and say them:

> sh__ld
> f___ld
> f___rce
> p___ce

These are all ei words, because the ei sound comes after c and it rhymes with me:

> receive
> deceive

Put ei into these words and say them:

> c___ling
> perc___ve
> conc___ve

When e and i are together and they do not rhyme with me, they are always written ei:

weigh

height

leisure

Put ei into these words and say them. You may need a grown up to help you read some of them; there are some strange ones here!

for___gn

sl___gh

r___ndeer

n___ther

n___ghbour

Home Learn

Write three sentences using at least one of these words in each sentence:

weigh   receive   thief   chief   believe   reindeer

a) _____

b) _____

c) _____

Activity

Ask a grown-up or friend to read out some of the ie and ei words to you. Spell them out in big letters in the air. Keep your movements fluid and relaxed. Say the sounds as you write them. Keep your imaginary writing joined-up.

Check Your Progress!
The i Before e Rule
Turn to page 48 and put a tick next to what you have just learned.

Top Tip!
Remember to give your child lots of praise – they'll work so much better.

Parents Start Here...

Show your child how they can use this technique of chopping up compound words to read difficult words, as well as spell them.

Compound Words

We can spell compound words by cutting them into two smaller words:

somebody   ➡   some   +   body

Cut these compound words up:

suitcase	➡	suit	+	case
dustbin	➡	_____	+	_____
nobody	➡	_____	+	_____
football	➡	_____	+	_____
hairbrush	➡	_____	+	_____
tablecloth	➡	_____	+	_____
milkshake	➡	_____	+	_____
hamburger	➡	_____	+	_____
evergreen	➡	_____	+	_____
facecloth	➡	_____	+	_____
bedtime	➡	_____	+	_____

Put these words together to make compound words:

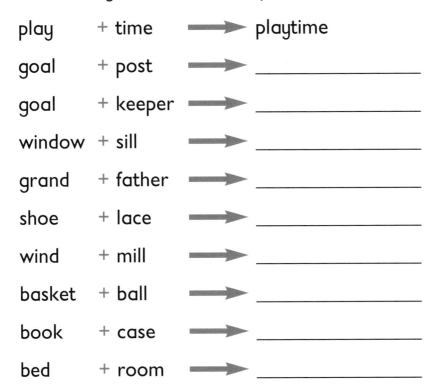

play + time → playtime

goal + post → _____

goal + keeper → _____

window + sill → _____

grand + father → _____

shoe + lace → _____

wind + mill → _____

basket + ball → _____

book + case → _____

bed + room → _____

Home Learn

Step One Look Say	Step Two Cover Write Check	Step Three Cover Write Check
dragonfly		
butterfly		
without		
nevertheless		
withstand		

What are the smaller words that make up each compound word?

Activity

Think up some more compound words – there are lots.

Check Your Progress!
Compound Words ☐

Turn to page 48 and put a tick next to what you have just learned.

31

Parents Start Here...

The National Literacy Strategy encourages learning at three different levels: word, sentence and text. Ensure your child continues to read a variety of books, especially those that challenge them.

Changing Verbs

Verbs are words that tell us what someone or something is doing or feeling.

Verbs can also tell us when something was being done, or felt.

The Present Tense

Verbs written in the present tense tell us what is happening now:

>   she is ironing
>   she irons

> **The Rule**: you add –ing or –s to verbs when you are writing in the present tense.

Write a correct form of the verb (present tense).

>   Verb: to walk
>   My Mum _____ to the shop.
>   Verb: to laugh
>   Mr Black _____at his dog.

The Past Tense

We often add the suffix –ed to verbs to show that something happened in the past.

>   I talk to her. ⟶ I talked to her.
>   She milks the cow. ⟶ She milked the cow.
>   The balloon floats. ⟶ The balloon _____.
>   A bulldozer flattens the car. ⟶ A bulldozer _____ the car.

Unfortunately, not all verbs are changed that easily. There are lots of exceptions you need to learn.

present		past	present		past
go	→	went	write	→	wrote
grow	→	grew	see	→	saw
buy	→	bought	build	→	built
bring	→	brought	sweep	→	swept
read	→	read **	kneel	→	knelt
			lend	→	lent
** (pronounced 'red')			sleep	→	slept

Home Learn

Match the present tense with the past tense

think	wove
weave	ran
run	led
teach	shook
shake	taught
steal	could
can	thought
rise	stole
lead	rose

Activity

Do you remember the rule for –ight? Can you think of a rule to help you remember –ought?

Check Your Progress!
Changing Verbs ☐
Turn to page 48 and put a tick next to what you have just learned.

33

Top Tip!
If your child struggles with anything, don't worry – let them go at their own pace.

Parents Start Here...

Spelling can be made a little more interesting by researching into the origins of words. A good etymological dictionary will help.

More Suffixes

Adding –al

We can add the suffix –al to a noun to change it into an adjective.

> A noun is a name, place or thing. An adjective describes a noun.

accident   ⟶   accidental

music   ⟶   _____

season   ⟶   _____

accident   ⟶   _____

post   ⟶   _____

origin   ⟶   _____

Adding –ness

We can add the suffix –ness to turn an adjective into a noun:

> **The Rule**: if the word ends in consonant –y, replace the –y with –i, before adding –ness.

happy   ⟶   happiness

ready   ⟶   _____

clumsy   ⟶   _____

grumpy   ⟶   _____

silly   ⟶   _____

Adding –hood

We can add the suffix –hood to some words to change their meaning:

man   ➡️   manhood

knight   ➡️   _____

neighbour   ➡️   _____

Adding –ment

We can add the suffix –ment to turn some verbs into nouns:

> Remember: if the word ends in -y you may need to replace the –y with –i before you add the –ment.

move   ➡️   movement

govern   ➡️   _____

merry   ➡️   _____

Home Learn

Step One Look Say	Step Two Cover Write Check	Step Three Cover Write Check
government		
parliament		
Prime Minister		
ballot box		
voting		
council		

Activity

The word 'parliament' comes from the French verb 'parler'. Find out what parler means. We have another word, 'parley', which comes from the same source. Find its meaning too.

> ## Check Your Progress!
> ### More Suffixes ☐
> Turn to page 48 and put a tick next to what you have just learned.

Parents Start Here...

Encourage your child to think of other homophones and then help them compose a poem which includes their suggestions.

Activities

1. Circle the correct homophones

Mr Jones the gardener eight/ate his sandwiches by the gate/gait.

"I choose/chews a berry/bury for my pudding" he said. Mr Jones' voice was sounding horse/hoarse because he had a saw/sore throat. Suddenly the sky turned grey and it began two/too/to hail/hale.

Mr Jones fought/fort off/of the hail by waving his hands.

'I hate this whether/weather" he shouted aloud/allowed. Mr Jones grabbed his hat to cover his bear/bare head but before long he felt his hare/hair getting wet/whet again.

"I/eye need/knead a new hat" he fumed. "This one/won has got a whole/hole in it."

2. Put c in front of the words that start with the soft s sound (like circle). Put k in front of the words that begin with a hard k sound (like kite).

_ick

_elery   _itchen

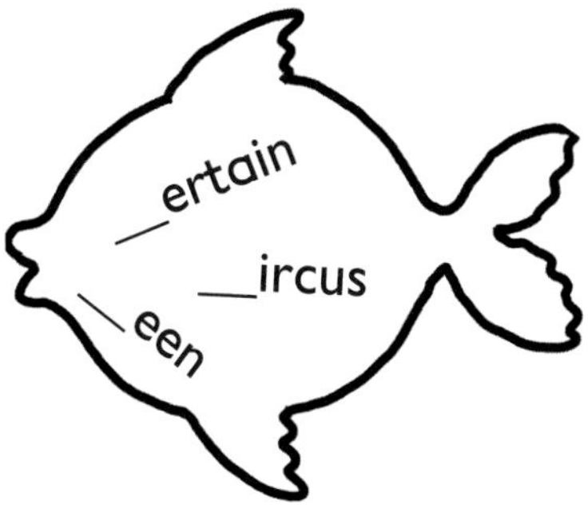

_ertain

_ircus

_een

_ell

_eep

_entury

3. Use these kn- words to complete the sentences:

knee   knuckle   knit   know   knife   knot   knack   knight

a) I used pink wool to _____ some socks for my Dad.

b) When Bob punched Mike he hurt his _____.

c) The _____ wasn't sharp at all.

d) There is a _____ to tying shoelaces.

Write four more sentences with the unused words:

e)

_____

f)

_____

g)

_____

h)

_____

37

Parents Start Here...

Ensure your child is still drinking water regularly throughout the day, eating balanced meals, exercising and sleeping well.

More Prefixes

A prefix is a group of letters that goes at the beginning of a word to change its meaning.

Earlier in the book we looked at the prefixes un–, dis– and re–.

Now we are going to look at the prefixes mis–, non–, anti–, inter– and pre–.

Adding mis–

The prefix mis– means bad, wrong or faulty.

mishap   misbehave   _____calculation   _____direct

Adding non–

The prefix non– means against or not.

nonsense   nonentity   _____flammable

Adding anti–

The prefix anti– means against.

antifreeze   _____clockwise

Adding inter–

The prefix inter- means among or between.

interview _____active _____net

Adding pre–

When you start looking, you will see prefixes everywhere. Even prefix has a prefix!

The prefix pre– means before.

prepare _____packaged _____dict _____arrange

Home Learn

Write three words that use each of these prefixes. Use a dictionary if necessary.

1. to– _____ _____ _____

2. over– _____ _____ _____

3. air– _____ _____ _____

Activity

You have probably used a number of words on this page that are new to you. Check their meanings in your dictionary.

Check Your Progress!

More Prefixes

Turn to page 48 and put a tick next to what you have just learned.

Top Tip! Bring what your child learns into everyday life – they'll remember it even better.

Parents Start Here...

Help your child find out whom July is named after.

Words To Learn

There are some important words you use again and again. You need to spell them properly.

Days Of The Week

Step One Look Say	Step Two Cover Write Check	Step Three Cover Write Check
Monday		
Tuesday		
Wednesday		
Thursday		
Friday		
Saturday		
Sunday		

Look out for the sneaky d in Wednesday.

What is the suffix used in every day of the week? _____

Months Of The Year

Remember that days of the week and months of the year always start with a capital letter.

Copy each word, using joined-up handwriting from beginning to end. You can dot your i s and cross your t s afterwards.

Top Spelling Tip: Look out for the extra r in February.

January	_____	July	_____
February	_____	August	_____
March	_____	September	_____
April	_____	October	_____
May	_____	November	_____
June	_____	December	_____

Home Learn

Saying a word in syllables (sounds) can help with the spelling. Say the word out loud and tap with your fingers to identify the syllables, then complete this table:

word syllable

recorder   rec/or/der
piano
violin
trumpet
cymbals
clarinet

Activity

The prefix oct- means eight (think of octopus or octagon). So why do you suppose the tenth month of the year begins with the Latin word for eight? Well, the Romans began their calendar in March. Find out what the Latin words 'novem' and 'decimus' mean. (You might be able to guess.)

Check Your Progress!
Words To Learn ☐
Turn to page 48 and put a tick next to what you have just learned.

Top Tip! Remember to give your child lots of praise – they'll work so much better.

Parents Start Here...

Encourage your child to start a Word Book or Word Bank, where they can collect all the words they frequently use.

Personal Details

When you fill in forms you may be asked to enter your 'personal details'.

Your personal details are your name, address, telephone number and date of birth.

Fill in this form. Ask a grown-up to explain the bits you're not sure about.

Title: Mr/Mrs/Miss/Ms/Dr ☐

Forename: _____

Surname: _____

Date Of Birth (dd/mm/yyyy): ☐ ☐ ☐

House Number: ☐

Street Name: _____

Town: _____

Postcode: _____

Telephone Number: _____

Email Address: _____

School Name: _____

School Address: _____

School Telephone Number: _____

If you don't know your school's telephone number you could find it in a telephone directory. This is a list of all the telephone numbers in your area.

Addressing Envelopes

Address this envelope to yourself:

Your name goes on the first line, followed by your address.

Put a comma at the end of each line until the last one, which you finish with a full stop.

Home Learn

Write yourself a Look, Say, Cover, Write and Check table and put in these words to learn:

school   computer   literacy   numeracy

exercise   address   assembly   science

primary

 # Activity

Think of any other words that are connected to school and write them on your chart.

Check Your Progress!
Personal Details ☐
Turn to page 48 and put a tick next to what you have just learned.

Top Tip!
Don't worry if your child does not understand straightaway – children learn at different speeds.

Parents Start Here...

Do not expect your child to be able to find words in the dictionary without some help from you. Talk them through the rules given here and practise together, using lots of different examples.

Using The Alphabet To List And Find Words

You will need your dictionary to hand for this page.

As you have worked your way through this book you have been using a dictionary. Here is a little more information on what dictionaries are, and how to use them.

Dictionaries

A dictionary is a collection of words that are written alphabetically. Dictionaries list the spellings and meanings of words.

- Etymological dictionaries also tell you where the words came from.

- Thesauruses contain lists of words that have similar meanings (synonyms) e.g. pretty, attractive, and beautiful.

- Rhyming dictionaries are helpful for writing poetry.

- Crossword dictionaries are great if you get stuck halfway through a crossword.

If you are going to use a dictionary you need to know your alphabet. Practise writing all the letters of the alphabet from a to z without taking your pen or pencil off the page:

abcdefghijklmnopqrstuvwxyz

You did this exercise at the beginning of the book. Has your writing improved since then?

Using A Dictionary

Do you know what the word puffball means? It sounds interesting, so let's look it up.

1. The word begins with p, so find p in your dictionary.
2. The next letter is u, so find entries beginning pu.
3. If you look at the top left hand side of each page you will see a word. This word is the first one listed on that page. e.g. pueblo.
4. If you look at the top right hand side of each page you will see another word. This word is the last one listed on that page e.g. pull.
5. You know that the third letter of your word (f) is between the third letters of these two words (e) and (l) so you are on the correct page.
6. Start at the top and look for words beginning puf–.

Write the meaning of puffball here: _____

Home Learn

Put these words in alphabetical order. Start with the first letters of each word. Words that start with the same letter can be ordered by putting the second letters in alphabetical order and so on.

orange	_____	black	_____
blue	_____	white	_____
yellow	_____	brown	_____
red	_____	purple	_____
pink	_____		

Activity

Keep a dictionary close at hand whenever you are working or writing. You will increase your vocabulary, improve your spelling and get much more enjoyment from your reading books.

Check Your Progress!
Listing And Finding Words
Turn to page 48 and put a tick next to what you have just learned.

Anagrams

Anagrams are new words that are made using all the letters from another word.

Join the words in red to their anagrams, but watch out — some have more than one anagram. One has been done for you.

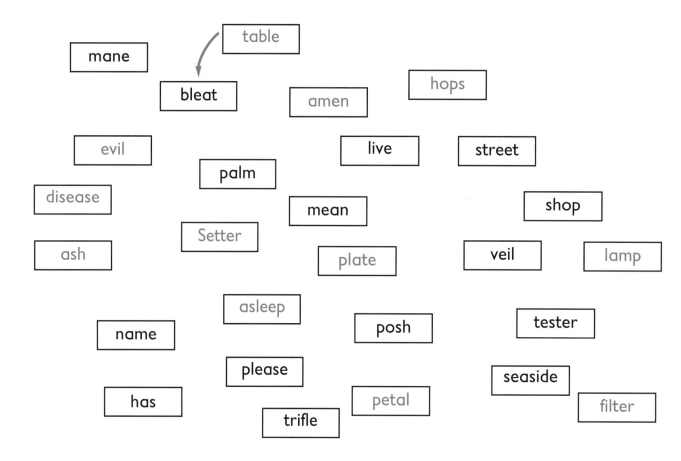

Think up your own anagrams for these words:

nap   _____

now   _____

rose   _____

pals   _____

reward   _____

pets   _____

stop   _____

Answers

Page 9
Home Learn
Some suggestions:
Anticlockwise, antihistamine
Antipodes, antiperspirant
Nonsense
Import, imprison
Inland, insane, indoors

Pages 10–11
brighter
brightest
closest
prettiest
sunny

Home Learn
milky
starry
skinny
furry
greasy

Pages 12–13
mates
foxes
buzzes
wishes
banjos
pianos
monarchs
shampoos
ratios
radios
Mondays
butties
lorries

Home Learn
planes
shoes
ostriches
emus
churches
keys
lollies
berries

Pages 18–19
kindly
nicely
quickly
clumsily
nastily
thoughtless – without thought
hopeless – without hope
luckless – without luck
homeless – without a home
thankless – without thanks
thankful
careful
disgraceful

Page 21
Home Learn
a) The train would've been
   on time.
b) I can't come to your house.
c) They aren't my friends
   any more.

Page 23
peace – piece
plane – plain
bored – board
sew – sow – so
here – hear
reign – rain
scent – sent
rode – road

Page 25
Brightly, boastfully and faithfully
are all adverbs.

Pages 28–29
shield
field
fierce
piece
ceiling
perceive
conceive
foreign
sleigh
reindeer
neither
neighbour

Pages 30–31
dust + bin
no + body
foot + ball
hair + brush
table + cloth
milk + shake
ham + burger
ever + green
face + cloth
bed + time

goalpost
goalkeeper
windowsill
grandfather
shoelace
windmill
basketball
bookcase
bedroom

Pages 32–33
Either of these examples
   is correct:
My Mum walks to the shop.
My Mum is walking to the shop.

Mr Black laughs at his dog.
Mr Black is laughing at his dog.

The balloon floated.
A bulldozer flattened the car.
Home Learn

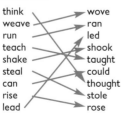

think	wove
weave	ran
run	led
teach	shook
shake	taught
steal	could
can	thought
rise	stole
lead	rose

Pages 34–35
musical
seasonal
accidental
postal
original

readiness
clumsiness
grumpiness
silliness

knighthood
neighbourhood

government
merriment

Pages 36–37
Mr Jones the gardener ate his
sandwiches by the gate.
"I choose a berry for my pudding"
he said. Mr Jones' voice was
sounding hoarse because he had
a sore throat. Suddenly the sky
turned grey and it began to hail.

Mr Jones fought off the hail by
waving his hands.
"I hate this weather" he shouted
aloud. Mr Jones grabbed his hat to
cover his bare head but before long
he felt his hair getting wet again.

"I need a new hat" he fumed.
"This one has got a hole in it."

2. celery
cell
century
certain
circus
keen
keep
kick
kitchen

3. a) I used pink wool to knit
      some socks for my Dad.
   b) When Bob punched Mike he
      hurt his knuckle.
   c) The knife wasn't sharp at all.
   d) There is a knack to tying
      shoelaces.

Pages 38–39
miscalculation
misdirect
nonflammable
anticlockwise
interactive
internet
prepackaged
predict
prearrange

Home Learn
Suggested words:
1. Today, tomorrow, tonight
2. Overbearing, overwrought,
   overly, overcoat, overact,
   overcast.

3. Airborne, airplane, airport.

Page 41
Home Learn
pi/a/no
vi/o/lin
trum/pet
cym/bals
cla/ri/net

Pages 44–45
black
blue
brown
orange
pink
purple
red
white
yellow

Page 46

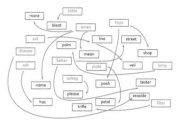

Anagrams:
nap = pan
now = own = won
rose = sore
pals = slap
reward = drawer = warder
pets = step
post = stop = pots

Check Your Progress!

How To Spell... ✓

Spelling With –ing And -le.. ☐

Common Prefixes... ☐

Changing Words... ☐

Writing Plurals .... ☐

Silent Letters... ☐

Changing The Meaning Of Words.. ☐

Apostrophes .... ☐

Homophones .... ☐

Common Letter Patterns .... ☐

The i Before e Rule.. ☐

Compound Words .... ☐

Changing Verbs .... ☐

More Suffixes.. ☐

More Prefixes .... ☐

Words To Learn .... ☐

Personal Details .... ☐

Listing And Finding Words .... ☐